Chrislight Kurt Léonel Zegue

Study and implementation of a ChatBot solution

Chrislight Kurt Léonel Zegue

Study and implementation of a ChatBot solution

ScienciaScripts

Imprint

Any brand names and product names mentioned in this book are subject to trademark, brand or patent protection and are trademarks or registered trademarks of their respective holders. The use of brand names, product names, common names, trade names, product descriptions etc. even without a particular marking in this work is in no way to be construed to mean that such names may be regarded as unrestricted in respect of trademark and brand protection legislation and could thus be used by anyone.

Cover image: www.ingimage.com

This book is a translation from the original published under ISBN 978-620-2-28281-9.

Publisher:
Sciencia Scripts
is a trademark of
Dodo Books Indian Ocean Ltd. and OmniScriptum S.R.L publishing group

120 High Road, East Finchley, London, N2 9ED, United Kingdom
Str. Armeneasca 28/1, office 1, Chisinau MD-2012, Republic of Moldova, Europe
Printed at: see last page
ISBN: 978-620-5-87583-4

Dedication

To my father **Jérémie Leopold ZEGUE**

My mother **Zoé Eliane MEGBLETO**

My brothers and sisters

Acknowledgements

Our first thanks go to our teachers at IFRI for their contribution to our training.

Secondly, we would like to thank our supervisors Mr Fréjus A.A **LALEYE**, teacher at IFRI and Mr Ronald **HOUKPONOU** for their precious recommendations and their availability.

Finally, we would like to thank all those who have contributed to this work.

Table of contents

API Application Programming Interface

CSRF Cross-Site Request Forgery

HTTP HyperText Transfer Protocol

MVT Model View Template

NLP Natural Processing Language

REST Representational State Transfer

SQL Structured Query Language

TALN Natural Language Processing

API: Application Programming Interface is a standardised set of classes, methods or functions that serves as a front end through which software offers services to other software.

CSRF: Cross-Site Request Forgery, abbreviated to CSRF (sometimes pronounced sea-surfing) or XSRF, is a type of vulnerability in web authentication services.

Framework: A set of components used to create the foundation, architecture and outline of a software product, a toolkit designed by one or more developers for other developers

ORM: object-relational mapping

REST: Representational State Transfer is an architectural style for designing networked applications

Summary

This paper presents the implementation and design of a conversational agent capable of dialoguing with humans in a transparent way on a given topic. In this paper we present the solution which is summarized in the realization of a platform of construction of a conversational agent. This platform with an API facilitates the design of a chatbot without worrying about how the processing is done at the level of the conversational robot. Thus, from a list of conversations, the conversational agent will learn to respond to users thanks to language processing based on automatic learning of the knowledge base.

Keywords: *API, conversational agent, machine learning.*

General introduction

Man's need to improve his way of life drives him every day to design technologies that can help him in certain fields including medicine, commerce, business industry and others. This insatiable need has led to the development of mobile platforms such as WhatsApp and Facebook Messenger, whose ultimate functionality is the sharing of information through messaging. In order to improve their way of communicating, conversational agents or chatbots were born, which are robots, intelligent machines capable of conversing with a human in a language that allows them to understand their needs. The concept of conversational agents was born in the 1950s but has gained momentum in the last two years due to technological advances.

Large companies such as IBM, Facebook, Twitter, Google and others have seen their importance. These companies promote their diffusion by opening platforms for developers. Chatbots have thus become indispensable in customer relationship management.

In this work, it is our task to make an inventory of the available open source chatbot solutions in order to implement an open source solution from an offered platform. In addition, we have created a generic chatbot API (Application Programming Interface) that can be integrated into any application to help the customer with his query or request.

This work will be in three main parts, a presentation of the study context and the inventory of existing solutions, an analysis and design of the chatbot solution and the implementation of the API and the chatbot solution.

Chapter 1

Study context and literature review

Introduction

This literature review is a retrospective of the various productions on the theme. It presents the generality and an inventory of existing solutions.

1.1 Issue

Today, the majority of social networking platforms are those that include instant chat features. In the past, when we had a question about a product, a comment about a service or an after-sales service to contact, we called a call centre. But with today's influential applications, it is now common practice to engage with brand community managers directly on Twitter or Facebook, to express dissatisfaction or to get quick and accurate information on a topic. Both of these solutions are likely to be relegated to memory and replaced by another form of instant messaging on our favourite social networks.

In order to satisfy their customers, many institutions, such as banks and insurance companies, create applications that incorporate instant chats, which allow them to respond in real time to people who need clarification or information about services they provide to the public.

The fact is that in order to be able to dialogue with an agent in the structure, the agent would have to be connected. A problem of efficiency and customer satisfaction quickly arises. First of all, the user has to wait for a connected agent, so if there is no connected agent, this is a hindrance to satisfying the request.

In this sense, we decided to study existing chatbot solutions in order to

build a Chatbot API and implement a chatbot solution that can interact with the user to address their concerns.

To carry out this work, we were hosted by Open Si as part of our end of cycle internship. Open Si is an expertise and consulting company on information and communication technologies.

1.2 Objectives

Many companies use conversational agents to offer personalised assistance to their customers in order to compensate for any failed customer experience. The main objective of this work is to set up, from a study of existing solutions, a chatbot for the company SAHAM Assurance Benin in order to :

- manage customer relations;
- allow any client to have an answer to his request even without the presence of a connected

agent;
- to historicise all questions in order to create a FAQ (Frequently Asked Questions);
- analyse needs to improve the SAHAM Assurance Benin system.

Specifically, it will be a question of creating a generic scavenger platform with an API. This implies :
- the integration of an Automatic Natural Language Processing (NLP) process for language understanding;
- storage of user information in a database;
- the creation of web services to access the data offered by the backend;
- securing the API.

1.3   General information on chatbots

A bot is a program that automatically interacts with a user. The coffee machine is a simple example: you press a button and it automatically makes coffee. Thus, during a conversation, the bot intervenes by responding to one human instead of another. The notion that is in the news and that now makes it an essential force in UX (User Experience) is that of a bot capable of integrating itself into a conversation: the chatbot. This is what makes the difference between a simple links and results program and a library of automated questions and answers.

The use of chatbots today is one of the keys to the success of digital customer relations. Today, fifty five percent (55%) of Internet users use instant messaging. For today's generation, webchat and social networking are the primary contact channels. Bots open up huge opportunities to enrich and even reinvent the User Experience (UX), they are the natural extension of virtual assistants.

There are four main families of chatbots:
- the chatbot that provides a specific service to the user,
- the chatbot that provides an experience,
- the commercial chatbot, carries out a commercial action,
- the entertainment chatbot, works as entertainment.

The operation of a chatbot is divided into three parts. First, the user uses a keyboard or a microphone to ask a question. Then the chatbot receives the information and analyses it through a web interface or an application interface. This understanding stage includes intention detection and is the engine of the chatbot. The third step consists in analysing the question. The chatbot consults its database to provide the most appropriate answer. To summarise, on the one hand we have the interface (e.g. Facebook, Slack, Skype) with a recognition of intentions or parameters thanks to machine learning. Then the chatbot engine takes into account customer-related scenarios.

Chatbots provide functionalities to be integrated into an application, but cannot replace it. Indeed, in 2016 there were more than 30,000 chatbots in Facebook's Messenger application alone[ ].

1.4 Presentation of existing solutions

Program O

Program O is an AIML interpreter written in PHP, and uses a MySQL database to store chatbot information, including the AIML files used to formulate chatbot responses[1] .
Program O requires PHP version 5.3.0 or higher to run. Its script has been tested with various server software, including Apache 1.3 and IIS (Internet Information Services) on Windows Millenia machines, with versions

1.   source :Official website of Program O : *https //program-o.com/*

MySQL server 5.0 and higher.
Program O also supports the creation of multiple chatbots. The bots are configured from an administrator platform. Bot-specific variables are stored in the database.
For botmasters and advanced programmers, it is possible to use the Program O API to access a chatbot from standalone applications viaHTTP[ ] requests.

APLai

This API provides speech to text and text to speech with learning capability, pre-built entities such as date and unit-currency, supports platforms such as Facebook, Slack and other messaging APIs[ ].

Wit.ai

The Wit.ai API is a completely free conversational agent design platform for public and private instances with no limitations on the rate of demand. It offers a nice combination of speech recognition and machine learning for developers, with support for various messaging APIs and SDKs.

MS Bot Framework

The MS Bot Framework is a conversational agent design platform that allows you to build and connect intelligent bots to interact with users, no matter where they are, through text, SMS, Slack, Office 365 mail and other popular services[H].

Motion AI

Motion AI is a platform for creating, training and deploying robots in a visual way with support for robust read and write APIs[12].

TABLE 1.1 - Comparative table of existing solutions

Bot	Langagev of programming - applications - integration	license	languages	channels	areas
API.ai	SDKs : An- droid, iOS, Cor-dova,HTML, Javascript, Nodejs, .NET, Unity, Xamarin, C++, python, Ruby, PHP, java, BotKit	free	English, French, Spanish, Russian, German, Turkish, Chinese, Korean, Italian, Japanese	Facebook, slack, twilo, telegram, kik, LINE, Skype, twitter, Alexa	conversational agent platform, services, appli cation and devices
MS Bot Framework	C# SDK, Python SDK, Node js SDK, Android SDK, Bot connec-tor , developer portal	Open Source and available on GitHub	automatic translation in over 30 languages	Facebook me-senger, slack, skype, website and other popular services	To be used to build high quality robots
wit.ai	node js client, python client, ruby client and other HTTP platforms	free	50 languages	Speech to text	used by over 65,000 developers to build messaging applications
Motion AI	node, java, python, iOS, Unity	free, standard, premium	English, Japanese	voice, image, text	doctor, finance, fantasy football, justice

Table 1.1 shows a comparison of existing solutions. The comparison is based on programming language, licence, operating language, channel and application area.

Conclusion

In this chapter, following the presentation of the existing solutions, it becomes clear that all API providers are still relatively new, as chat bots are just starting to attract public attention. To date, API.ai seems to be the leader in this field. Since it easily integrates into almost all platforms and technologies Java, Javascript, Android, Cordova, Node.js, WebKit HTML5, Python, iOS, Ruby, Php, C++, .Net (C#) etc. . Nevertheless, we opt for the design of an own platform to generate a chatbot. Because our structure has clients such as banks, the state, insurance companies and other private institutions that have sensitive data specific to their clients. Therefore we cannot afford to store this sensitive data in databases other than our own. Finally, it will be useful for us to integrate our own functionality into the platform.

Chapter 2
Analysis and design of the chatbot solution

Introduction

In this chapter, we present the analysis, modelling and design of our solution using the UML method. In the analysis phase, we describe the user requirements in detail. In the design phase, we provide more details on the proposed solution, and we seek to clarify the technical aspect of the work.

2.1 Analysis

Requirements analysis and specification is the first phase of the software development cycle. They serve to identify the reactive actors of the system[ ]. Thus, the actual requirements of our application are as follows:

- Sending responses instantly to the user;

- understanding the natural language of users;

- full flexibility of application.

Design is the third step of the V-Design cycle. During this design phase we modelled the functionality of our application. To do this, we chose the *Unified Modeling* Language (UML) which is a pictogram-based graphical modelling language designed to provide a standardised method. UML allows the design of a system to be visualised. It is commonly used in software development. The modelling of our system is based on the following diagrams:

- the use case diagram ;

- the sequence diagram ;

- the activity diagram.

2.1.1 Use case diagram

Use case diagrams are used to give an overall view of the functional behaviour of a software system. They are useful for presentations to the management or stakeholders of a project.

Identification of actors

The actors of a system are the entities that are external to the system and that interact with it. These actors make it possible to define the interface that the system will have to offer to its environment. The actors of our system are the **Users**.

Use cases

Use cases describe exhaustively the functional requirements of the system. Each use case corresponds to a business function of the system from the point of view of one of its actors. Here there are three use cases: **account creation, authentication** and **sending a request** for a receipt.

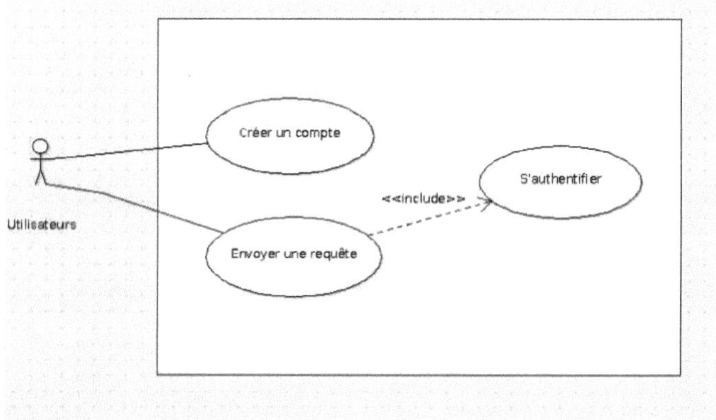

FIGURE 2.1 - Use case diagram

2.1.2 Sequence diagram

A sequence diagram is a UML (Unified Modeling Language) diagram that represents the sequence of messages between objects during an interaction. A sequence diagram consists of a group of objects, represented by lifelines, and the messages that these objects exchange during the interaction. Sequence diagrams represent the sequence of messages passed between objects. They can also represent the control structures between objects.

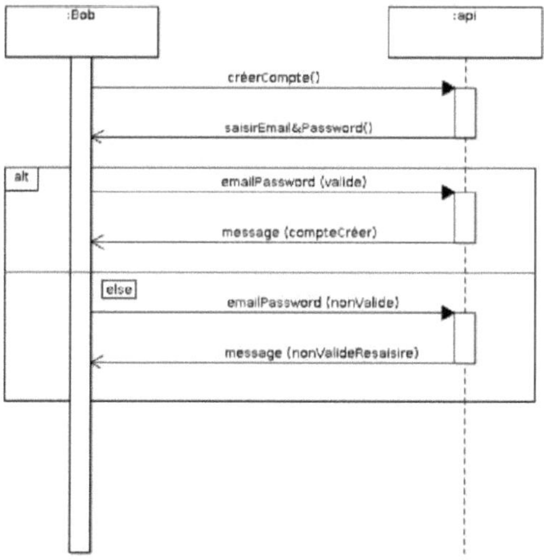

FIGURE 2.2 - Sequence diagram of the create an account use case

The diagram below relates the sequence diagram of the *create an account* use case.

User scenario	Operations at the system level
the user requests to create an account	the system asks the user to enter their

	email and password pass.
the user enters their email and a password	1. the system performs a check of the email. 2. the email is correct, the system sends a confirmation message to both the mailbox and the platform.

TABLE 2.1 - Successful account creation scenario

1. the system performs a check of the email.
2. the email is incorrect, the system performs the result of the first scenario.

the user enters their email and a password

TABLE 2.2 - Successful account creation error scenario

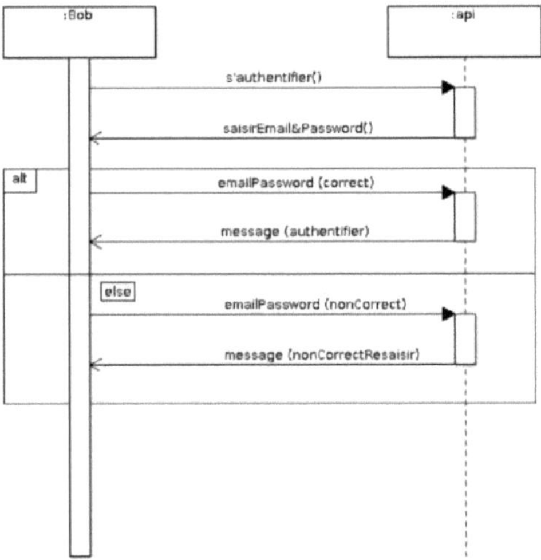

FIGURE 2.3 - Authenticate use case sequence diagram

User	Back-end/API
the user sends a request	1. the system checks the token client authentication. 2. the system sends a response back to the user.

TABLE 2.3 - Request sending scenario

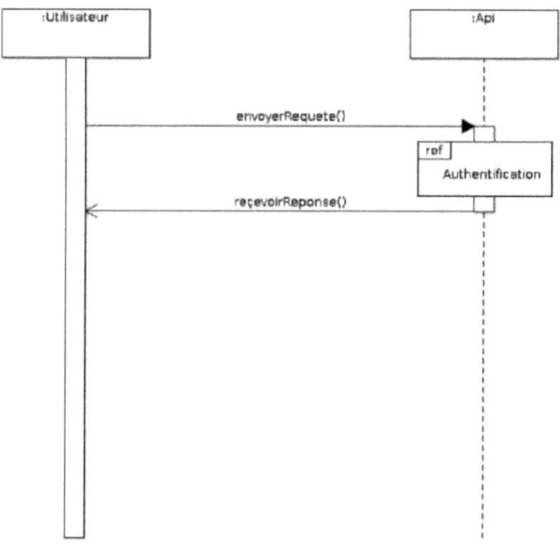

FIGURE 2.4 - Sequence diagram of the send request use case

2.2 System architecture

We have adopted an N-tier client-server architecture. In this architecture, we have the API component, whose role is to provide in the form of services the functionality required by the business logic. There are three main components in our system architecture:

- ° the user interface through which users can interact with the bot;

- ° the engine that processes user messages (Backend), with a database to store user-related data;

- ° the Natural Language Processing engine, which transforms user input into actions that can be executed by the engine.

This structure resembles a classic architecture with a Frontend and a Backend that exposes an API. The main difference is the presence of the NLU (Natural Language Understanding) engine.

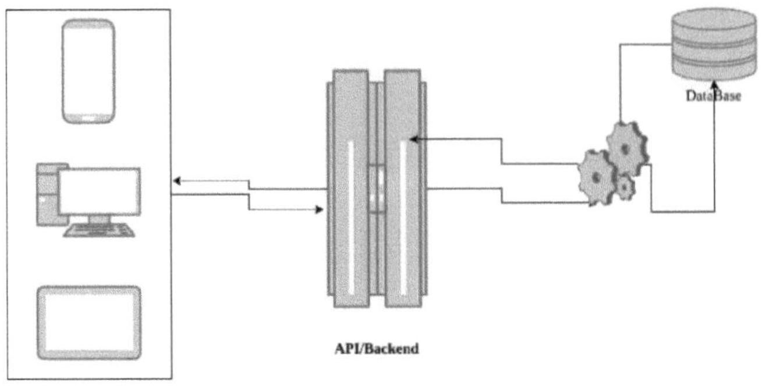

FIGURE 2.5 - System architecture

2.2.1 Machine learning process

The chatbot includes tools that help simplify the learning process. This process involves loading a sample dialog box into the chatbot's database. This builds on the data structure that represents the known instruction and response sets. When the chatbot's learning module is subjected to a dataset, it creates the necessary entries in the bot's knowledge graph so that the inputs and responses to a query are correctly represented.

Figure 2.6 shows two different conversations but in the same context. These two conversations represent lists of inputs sent to the system. Then, the bot, in order to train itself, makes an association between the inputs having the same context to form a knowledge graph as shown in Figure 2.6 .

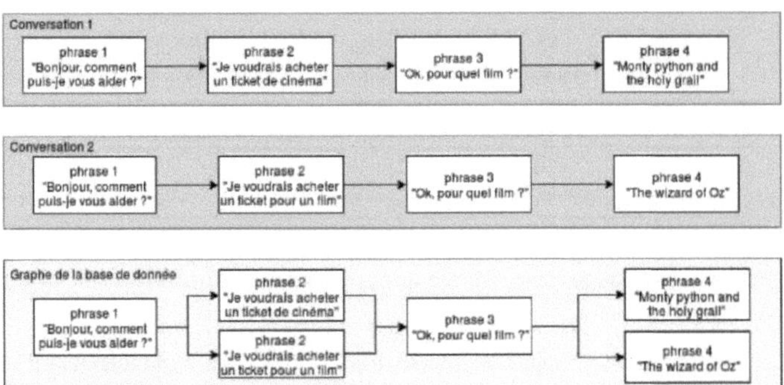

FIGURE 2.6 - Training process graph

2.2.2 Description of our API modules

2.2.2.1 Integration of an NLP process

Automatic Natural Language Processing (NLP) is an essential task in the creation of a chatbot. It consists of integrating into the robot the way to process the information received by the users.

Automatic language processing is a discipline at the frontier of linguistics, computer science and artificial intelligence. It provides a computational treatment of human language based on computer techniques applied to all aspects of human language. It is used to analyse text and allows the robot to understand how humans interact. Text analysis includes sentiment analysis, topic extraction, named entity recognition, relationship extraction etc.

Figure 2.7 shows the syntactic analysis of the sentence I *would like to buy some clothes*. The processing of this simple sentence reveals 5 properties as follows:

- the *dependency* which represents the different relationships between each word in the sentence;

- the *part ofspeech* which represents the grammatical analysis of the sentence (verb, pronoun, determiner, noun);

- the *lemma* which identifies the correspondence of certain words in the sentence with verbs and other words;

- *morphology*, which makes a grammatical analysis of each word in the sentence;

- the *parse label*, which makes an identification by keyword.

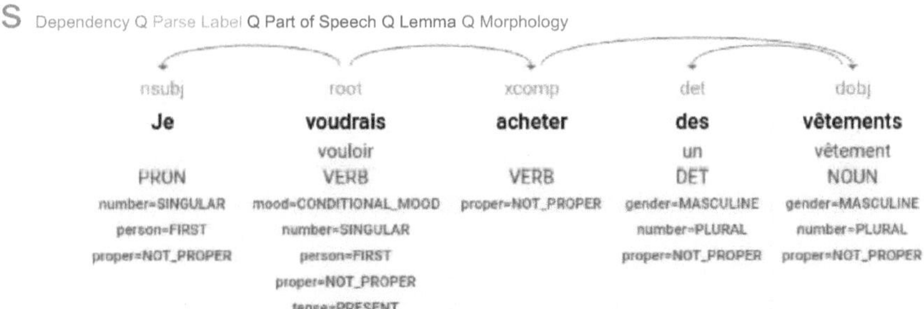

FIGURE 2.7- Scheme of a syntactic analysis by TALN

Thus, all these elements and others are taken into account when the NLP analyses a sentence. This is how the bot identifies the context of a sentence.

2.2.2.2 Storing user information in a database

At this stage the user information i.e. the conversation lists are stored in the database, as well as the user information such as email and password.

2.2.2.3 Creation of web services to access the data offered by the backend

A web service is a computer program that enables communication and data exchange between heterogeneous applications and systems in distributed environments. It is therefore a set of functionalities exposed on the Internet or on an intranet, by and for applications or machines, without human intervention, and in real time. In other words, a web service is simply a program that is accessible via the Internet, uses a standard XML (*Extensible Markup Language)* messaging system and is not tied to any operating system or programming language. Here we have used the REST (*Representational State Transfer*) architecture which is a web services architecture. REST is a way of building an application for distributed systems like the World Wide Web. Thus, at this level we offer users the possibility to communicate with the bot through other applications.

2.2.2.4   Securing the API

As long as we have to move information between different networks and interconnect different applications we should take security measures to minimise security breaches.

Below we have classified the measures we have adopted according to the principles of IT security:

Confidentiality

Confidentiality is the act of ensuring that information is only accessible by those entities that have the right to access it. The system we have developed integrates an access role management module. Indeed, users wishing to access the information offered by the API must first authenticate themselves.

Authenticity

Within an information system, it is important to verify the authenticity of each resource. This is possible thanks to the authentication mechanism, which makes it possible to prove the identity of a person through the identification process.
First of all, before calling any URL, you must authenticate yourself. We avoid circulating the user's login parameters. Instead we used a token which is a long string of characters generated and encrypted automatically when the user authenticates. It is now this renewable, time-limited key that is sent along with requests to authenticate the user. Any request that does not contain a token or contains invalid tokens is automatically rejected.

Conclusion

Throughout this chapter, we have identified the different actors in the system. We have also identified the different use cases and proceeded to draw the different diagrams. We have also described the machine learning process.

Chapter 3

Implementation of the API and chatbot

Introduction

After the analysis and design steps presented in the previous chapter, all that remains is to present a description of the implementation process and the test scenarios of the API

3.1 Process of realising the API

In this section we will present the technologies and tools used for the implementation of our chatbot.

3.1.1 Programming tools

When researching the technologies suitable for the realisation of our bot, we found that there were two choices available to us, namely:

- develop our application with *Node js* which is an open source, event-driven JavaScript software platform oriented towards network applications that need to scale. It has very useful modules in the field of artificial intelligence.

- develop an application with *Flask* which is a python framework. *Python,* nowadays is considered as the reference language in the development of intelligent applications and contains very large libraries in the field of artificial intelligence.

Of these two possibilities we chose to use *Flask* because it offers more richness in terms of functionality, quality and performance thanks in part to the Python language. To develop our application, we used **PyCharm** which is an integrated development environment (IDE) created by JetBrain.

In addition, we needed a machine learning phase carried out using the *ai-chatbot-framework*[1] from python. *Ai-chatbot-framework is* a python framework that facilitates the generation of automated responses to a user. *Ai-chatbot-framework* uses a selection of machine learning algorithms to produce different types of responses. This allows developers to create chat bots and automate conversations with users. The language-independent design of the *ai-chatbot- framework* allows the bot to be trained to speak any language. In addition, the machine learning nature of the ai-chatbot-framework allows an agent instance to improve its own knowledge of possible responses as it interacts with humans and other sources of informative data. An instance of *ai-chatbot-framework* begins without knowing how to communicate. As *ai-chatbot-framework* receives more input, the number of answers it can deliver becomes considerable with precision on every answer given.

The program selects the closest matching response by searching for the closest corresponding known instruction that matches the input, and then chooses a response from the selection of known responses to that statement. In order to implement the API for our application we used *REST. REST* will allow us to move purely towards an API describing the resources used in our Flask application. The great advantage of using a REST API is that it allows a separation between client and server. Thus multiple clients can be developed to consume the resources made available by the API. The great advantage of *REST* is that it allows the API to be requested with simple *HTTP* requests. *GET* requests will retrieve resources, *POST* requests will modify them, and *DEEETE* requests will delete them. Of course, our application has a web interface that allows the user to create an account, connect and test the bot. Thus, in the realization of this interface we used *Materialize css* which is a CSS framework (*Cascading Style Sheets*).

This part ends with the presentation of **Git**, a tool that has been at the heart of our development work. Since we need a version manager, we chose *Git* which is a decentralised version management software. It is free software created by Linus Torvalds, author of the Linux kernel, and distributed under the terms of the GNU General Public License version 2. In 2016, it became the most popular version management software, used by more than twelve million people[ ]. As an online repository, we used the community version of *Gitlab* with private repositories.

1. *https ://github.com/alfredfrancis/ai-chatbot-framework*

1.1.2 Database engine

To store the data processed by our system we chose to use a NoSQL database. As a NoSQL database, we chose mongoDB. MongoDB is a robust and powerful database management system with rich and advanced features, capable of handling large volumes of data reliably. It is extremely standards compliant. The main reason for our focus on mongoDB is that it is open-source, and is developed by a global community of thousands of developers and dozens of companies. This allows us, unlike a proprietary solution, to avoid licensing costs for the project. In addition, mongoDB is a concurrent database management system, which means that several users can perform operations simultaneously.

1.1.3 Software architecture

During the realisation of our project we used a software architecture standard. This is the MVT (*Model View Template*) architecture. The **Model** represents information stored somewhere, most often in a database. It allows access to the information, to modify it, to add new information, to check that it corresponds to the criteria (we speak of the integrity of the information), to update it, etc. It is an additional interface between our code and the database. The **View** is, as its name suggests, the visualisation of the information. It is the only thing the user can see. Not only is it used to present a piece of data, but it is also used to collect a possible action from the user (a click on a link, or the submission of a form for example). Typically, an example of a view is a web page, nothing more, nothing less. Finally, the **Template** represents an HTML file, also called a "template". It will be retrieved by the view and sent to the visitor. However, before being sent, it will be parsed and executed by the framework, as if it were a file with code.

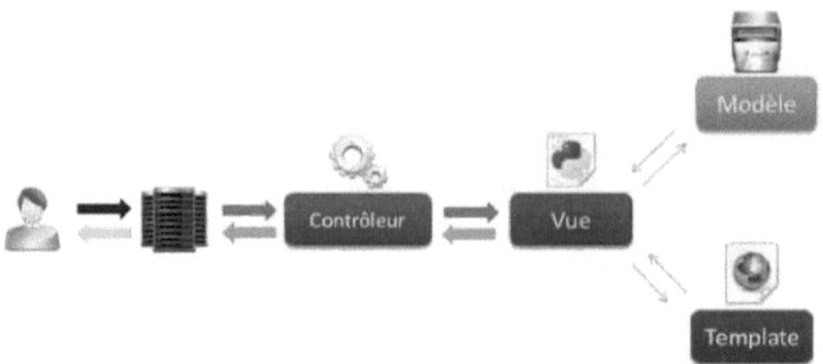

FIGURE 3.1 - Query execution diagram

3.2 Presentation of the platform

The platform is subdivided into six main interfaces, the *user registration interface*, the *login interface*, the *user profile*, the *user intention creation interface*, the *training interface* and the *robot test interface*. The registration interface (Figure 3.2) of a user presents four fields, the user's *name*, *first name*, *email* and a *password*.

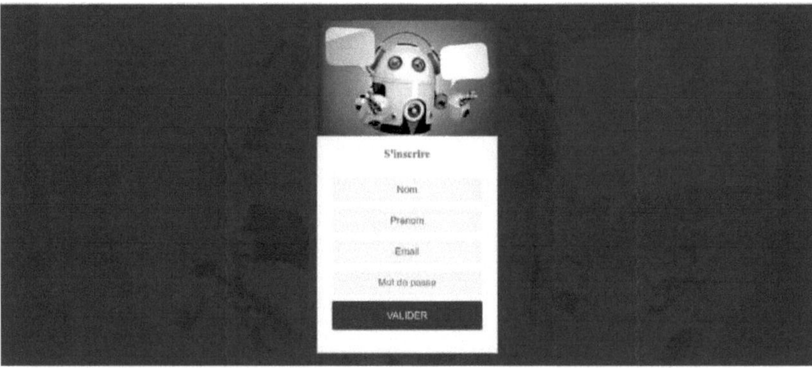

FIGURE 3.2 - User registration interface

The login interface (Figure 3.3) has two fields, *email* and *password*.

FIGURE 3.3 - Testing the api response reception service

After validating these two interfaces, the user profile is accessed, which is the interface for creating a conversational agent (Figure 3.4). To create an agent, simply press the create an agent button and fill in the fields.

For the conversational agent configurations, click on the *open* link.

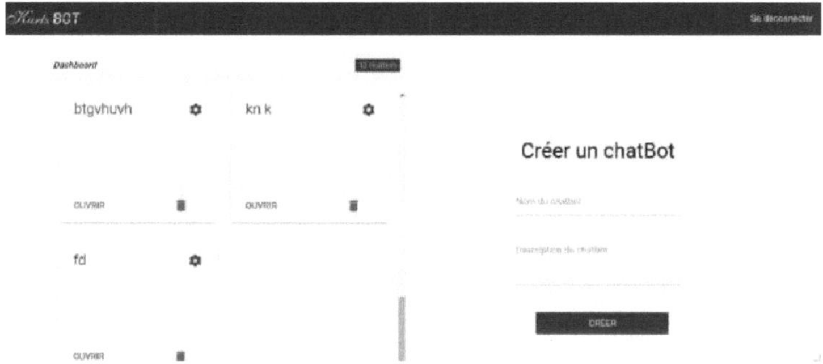

FIGURE 3.4 - Testing the api response reception service

The intention creation interface has two sections, one for creation and the other for the list of intentions created. To create an intention, simply fill in the fields: *context, intention name*. If the intention contains values that the conversational robot must retrieve to respond to a user, then the *parameter* field must be filled in and a default message defined if this parameter is not available. Finally, the possible response(s) of the robot in relation to this intention must be filled in.

FIGURE 3.5 - Testing the api response service

Each created intent has a *train* button, which allows to go to the robot training interface for the intent. At this level, the possible inputs of a user must be put in and the *START LABELING* button must be pressed to start an analysis of this input into normed entities. If the input contains a value to be retrieved by the bot, select this value with the mouse and enter the parameter that defines it. Then press *ADD TO TEST SET* to save. Perform this process as desired for different user inputs. Finally press *BUIL MODEL* to build the conversation model.

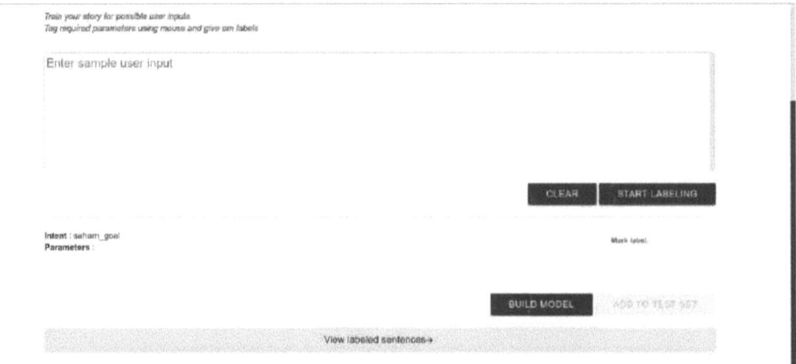

FIGURE 3.6 - Testing the api response reception service

3.3 API test scenario

At this stage, we present the API through a tool, *Postman*, which is an API testing tool. In order to receive responses from the chat bot through other applications other than our web platform we have created an address through which users can receive a response to their question. Figure 3.7 illustrates this scenario:

FIGURE 3.7 - Testing the api response reception service

We notice at this level that the user makes a POST on the url `/api/v1` *(I want information on saham assurance)* as shown in figure 3.7 in **1** and then the bot sends him an answer in **2** (*the Saham Assurance group works to meet the essential needs of the person...*). Indeed, to have access to the API, it is necessary to send an *apiKey*, an *input* which represents the input of a user, *a complete* which takes the value *true* in a JSON format (application/json).

3.4 Presentation of the Saham Assurance Benin chatbot

Through our platform we have developed a chatbot for Saham Assurance Benin. Indeed, the bot currently has knowledge related to the objectives of Saham Assurance, their services and information about each of them.

FIGURE 3.8 - Presentation of the chatbot

Conclusion

In this chapter, we have presented our system, through screenshots of the different test scenarios. Our system thus presented meets the specified needs but has some shortcomings.

General conclusion

This report presents the results of our work done during our internship as part of our Bachelor's degree project in Software Engineering. During this 3-month internship, we were able to put into practice our theoretical knowledge acquired during our training. Moreover, we managed to execute the basic functionalities that had been submitted to us within the deadlines, even though we had experienced some difficulties. After our quick integration into the *Open Si* team, the host company, we learned to work with new procedures and constraints to develop our chatbot solution.

We started our study with a needs analysis, which is a crucial and necessary step to better understand the existing situation. Then we proceeded to the conceptual analysis through a basic architecture, which is the starting point of the design. Finally we proceeded to the justified choice of technologies before moving on to the implementation, which allowed us to develop the application and the API taking into account the hardware architecture and the software environment.

It is difficult to claim to have had an ideal solution, but we hope to have addressed our problem. However, we are aware that there is room for improvement. We plan to expand our vision of things by integrating other artificial intelligence functionalities to our chatbot thanks to cloud services such as voice recognition, interaction with data other than the user's. We also plan to integrate a functionality allowing the bot to make automatic summaries of results in order to better guide a user. Expand the knowledge base of the Saham Assurance Benin chatbot.

Bibliography

[1] Shawar B.A., *A Corpus Based Approach to Generalising a Chatbot System*, 2011.

[2] Steven Bird, Ewan Klein, Edward doper, *Natural Language Processing with Python*, 2009.

[3] Laurent AUDIBERT, *UML2 From learning to practice*, 2009.

[4] Peltier, Mathieu *Developing Web applications with the django 2 framework*, 2009.

[5] POREBSKI, Bartosz, PRZYSTALSKI, Karol, and NOWAK, Leszek. *Buildingpython Applications with Django*. John Wiley and Sons, 2013.

Webography

[6] *sourcewikipedia,* `https://fr.wikipedia.org/wiki/Cycle en V.`Accessed06May2017

[7] *source wikipedia,* https://fr.rn.wikipedia.org/wiki/Git. Accessed on 04 May 2017

[8] Official *GitHub, Inc.* website *[US],* https://github.com/Program-0/Program-0. Accessed 03 May 2017

[9] *Google's API.ai platform,* https://api.ai/.Consulté on 07 May 2017

[10] Official website of *Wit.ai,* https://wit.ai/. Accessed on 07 May 2017

[11] Microsoft Bot Framework https://dev.botframework.com/. Accessed on 15 May 2017

[12] *Motion ai* website, https://www.motion.ai/. Accessed 19 May 2017

[13] *Defabernovel* website, `https://www.fabernovel.com/insights/tech/comprendre-les-chatbots.` Accessed May 24, 2017

[14] *Natural Language Toolkit* website, www.nltk.org/. Accessed 29 May 2017

[15] *Chatterbot* website, `http://chatterbot.readthedocs.io/en/stable/testing.html.` Accessed 26 May 2017

[16] *ai-chatbot-framework* website, `https://github.com/alfredfrancis/ai-chatbot- framework.` Accessed on 6 June 2017

Printed by Books on Demand GmbH, Norderstedt / Germany